Yᵉ AGAPEMONE. WITH·A·PROSPECTE OF ᵗʰᵉBROTHERS AND·SISTERS. A PLAYINGE· AT HOCKEY.– ALSO ᵗʰᵉBROTHER Sᵛᵗ·MISTER·PRINCE bᵞˢ 4 IN HANDE.

West Country Scandals

James Whinray

Bossiney Books

Some other recent Bossiney titles which might interest you

Brunel in the West
Dartmoor's history
Devon festivals
Denon's seaside history
Druids in the South-West?
Haunted inns of Devon
How Devon changed the world – a bit
Spies, lies and books
Tales from Devon folklore
Walking the South Devon coast in 1854
Weirdest buildings of the South-West

The cover illustration is by Hugh Thompson (1860-1920) and was used in an edition of *The School for Scandal* in 1911. The title page illustration is from *Punch*, and refers to the Agapemonite scandal, see page 30.

First published 2018 by
Bossiney Books Ltd, 67 West Busk Lane, Otley, LS21 3LY
www.bossineybooks.com
© 2018 James Whinray   All rights reserved
ISBN 978-1-906474-67-6
Printed in Great Britain by R Booth Ltd, Penryn, Cornwall

The bigamous Duchess

The late Georgian era was an age of scandal, mainly involving the aristocracy and the theatre world – but the theatre had been acceptably scandalous from Nell Gwyn onward. As for the aristocracy, probably their morals were no worse than they had been, but as a writer in 1788 put it:

> This is an age when the prying eye of curiosity penetrates the privacy of every distinguished person; neither the living nor the dead escape.

Needless to say, that very same author, after bewailing the trend towards celebrity culture, immediately indulged himself by writing a striking example of it. His book was called *An authentic detail of particulars relative to the late Duchess of Kingston*.

The increase in Georgian scandal was brought about by the rise, from about 1770, of popular monthly publications such as *Town and Country Magazine*. Prior to that, journalists feared exposing aristocratic peccadilloes, but the mood rapidly changed. The newly affluent 'middling sort' were suddenly made aware of aristocratic behaviour, and were shocked – in some cases pleasurably shocked no doubt.

A rather strange old assumption that the crown and aristocracy were rightfully set over us because their members were morally superior was rapidly eroded.

Town and Country Magazine specialised in covering divorce cases. These had been very rare – an average of just one divorce a year – because of the enormous cost. They required a husband first to prove that his wife had committed adultery (wives had to prove much more, so they were rarely the plaintiff) by suing the co-respondent for damages. The courts required detailed evidence, mostly from servants describing sounds heard, or rumpled beds. That was then followed by a further case in the ecclesiastical courts, and then an Act of Parliament. All very expensive.

The court evidence was often titillating. If quoted verbatim it had the huge advantage for a journalist that there was no risk of libel. The increasing number of divorce cases was bread and butter to the magazines, but the scandal of the Duchess of Kingston was even better.

She was tried for bigamy by her peers in the House of Lords, something quite unprecedented.

Elizabeth Chudleigh (1721-1788) came from a Devon landowning family, based at Ashton just north of the town of Chudleigh. Her father Colonel Thomas Chudleigh, a younger son, had lost most of his money by investing in the South Sea Bubble and was mainly dependent on his £200 p.a. income, with lodging for the family provided, as Lieutenant-Governor of the Royal Hospital at Chelsea; but he died when Elizabeth was five, leaving the mother (born Henrietta Chudleigh, Thomas's first cousin) dependent on rents from Hall Farm at Ashton.

She and her children (only two survived from seven born) moved to Maddox Street Stable Yard in Mayfair, which sounds pretty bad, though more respectable if described as 'a mews house just off Bond Street'. To make ends meet they took in a female lodger: how humiliating.

But the family still had contacts. William Pulteney, a wealthy Whig politician who became 1st Earl of Bath, paid for Elizabeth to have some education and later found her a post as Maid of Honour to the Princess of Wales. This paid a salary of £200 p.a., which probably didn't cover the court dressmaker's bills, but did provide an opportunity for networking, and for the vital matter of attracting a rich husband.

Elizabeth was in her element. She was always the life and soul of the party, and quickly gained a reputation as a party organiser and later as a hostess in her own right. And she certainly attracted potential husbands, including the Duke of Hamilton. But he was only 19, his estate was in debt, and his trustees would have wished him to marry money, so perhaps he was not the right catch for Elizabeth, who had nothing.

If marriage was a necessity for a gentlewoman without a personal fortune (since there was virtually no paid employment available) it was almost as necessary for the male heirs of titled families. An heir to an estate was expected to ensure that he in turn had an heir. Both family and society generally put great presssure on him to marry early and have at least two sons (the heir and a spare) after which his life was his own. He must marry even if he was gay. Meanwhile younger sons could and did sow their wild oats.

For reasons that remain a mystery, Elizabeth was persuaded, apparently by her aunt Lady Ann Hanmer, to marry Augustus Hervey. He was a naval officer, younger son of the heir of the Earl of Bristol – his elder brother was quite sickly so his long-term prospects were quite good, but he had virtually no money at that time. Elizabeth's mother was apparently unaware of the marriage, and Hervey himself was a minor who had no parent present at the ceremony to give consent.

The wedding was conducted in secret so that Elizabeth could retain her status, and her income, as a Maid of Honour. It took place at night in a tumbledown chapel in Lainsty, Hampshire, a parish where there was only one house, which belonged to a cousin. There was just one candle to light the chapel and the clergyman mumbled the words because he could not read in the dark. Perhaps some words of the ceremony were omitted. There were just five other people present, one of them a servant.

After this thoroughly unsatisfactory episode the marriage was consummated and two days later Hervey left to join his ship at Portsmouth. It was two years before he returned, by which time for whatever reason Elizabeth wished never to see him again.

> She ran the career of pleasure, enlivened the Court circles, each year became more ingratiated with the mistress whom she served; led fashions; played whist with Lord Chesterfield; rioted with Lady Harrington and Miss Ashe; figured at a masquerade, and laughed at the lover whom she chose not to favour with her smiles, with all the confounding grace of a woman of quality.

It seems that because she was surreptitiously married, Elizabeth was obliged to reject a genuine proposal from the Duke of Hamilton, now of age, which must have been galling, and of course that refusal aroused the curiosity of society.

When Hervey returned from his voyage Elizabeth refused to

Elizabeth Chudleigh as Iphigenia at a private masquerade in 1749 – though this version probably owes much to tabloid press imagination

see him for two months, but finally had to give in. He locked her in a room and insisted on his marital rights. A son was born in secret (though the birth was attended by the Prince of Wales' personal surgeon) and baptised in Chelsea on 2 November 1747 as Augustus-Henry Hervey. The baptism was conducted by Hervey's uncle. As so often happened, the baby died aged just 11 weeks. Elizabeth returned to Court.

Hervey, who later became a very successful naval officer, paid some of her debts from his prize-money, but the marriage would never recover and she could not rely on him financially. Both of them were trapped. She only visited him when she wanted her debts cleared.

Elizabeth survived a mishap when a servant apparently confused a bottle of laudanum with a bottle of another medicine. Elizabeth swallowed a quantity which should have killed her. Her mother and a physician kept her awake by shaking her. It sounds rather like a suicide attempt.

Her notoriety with the press had been greatly increased by her appearance at a private masquerade in 1749, scantily clad – though perhaps not *quite* as scantily as later prints suggested. The sixty-six-year-old George II asked if he could put his hand on her breast. She replied that she could think of a much softer place, took his hand and positioned it on his head. The king gave her mother the post of housekeeper at Windsor (£350 p.a.), and publicly claimed a kiss from Elizabeth as his reward. The kiss was granted.

She was on her way to becoming a 'demi-rep' – a gentlewoman seen as only half reputable – and by 1752 she was the mistress of the Duke of Kingston-upon-Hull, who provided her with a large new-built house overlooking Hyde Park and the Serpentine. It was called Chudleigh House, 'but the vulgar beings say she lives in Concubine Row'. Well, the king's mistress lived next door but one.

She hosted parties for the royal family and foreign visitors, and soon there was gossip about her secret marriage and lost child. 'Maid of Honour' was a job description which caused a certain amount of hilarity.

The couple were apparently highly compatible, each enjoying

rural fishing trips and quiet time together, and the arrangement was both privately happy and publicly accepted for a number of years.

In 1775 Hervey, by now 3rd Earl of Bristol, decided he wanted his freedom, so that he could produce an heir. Rather than going through an expensive and painfully public divorce, Elizabeth suggested a legal fiction, a court action to prove no legal marriage had ever taken place. By this time she may well have convinced herself it had not.

Hervey was required to prove positively in an ecclesiastical court that the marriage had occurred. He (apparently) could not do so, and since she swore on oath there had been no marriage, the court decided the marriage had not happened.

So Elizabeth was, in law, free to marry the Duke of Kingston, which she duly did on her 48th birthday, 8 March 1769. The effect was not what she might have hoped. The social rejection was total. Whilst adultery was fine, bigamy was not. But the couple were in fact perfectly happy living away from London society, mostly at Thoresby Hall in the 'Dukeries' of Nottinghamshire but spending much time on holiday in the West Country, at Bath but also near Exeter and Plymouth.

Sadly the Duke died in 1773, without an heir. Elizabeth was heartbroken. Society being what it was, she was criticised for over-acting her grief. How could she *possibly* be sincere?

She travelled abroad, where she was well received by the Pope, the Electress of Saxony and Frederick the Great of Prussia. She was after all extremely rich, having inherited all the Duke's personal possessions and the income from his estates. (Apparently it helps to be both rich and titled.) She endeared herself to her sycophants by giving lavish presents: sometimes she later regretted this, as when she realised that she'd given away an original Raphael and a Claude Lorrain without appreciating their value – and promptly insisted she'd just asked the recipient to look after them for her.

Her first husband Hervey had chosen not to marry his long-term mistress, so he never had a legitimate heir. Members of his family who had a potential interest in his estate started digging around independently for evidence of his earlier marriage, which might give them access to Elizabeth's fortune. They were successful in locating the servant who had been present at the 'ceremony'. This woman had previously denied any memory of the event, but she had then applied to Elizabeth for a pension, and felt the offer of 20 guineas a year – especially with the added condition that she should live in Yorkshire – was unacceptable: her memory returned once a larger pension was within reach.

While Elizabeth was in Rome, she heard that she was to be subjected to a criminal trial for bigamy. If she was not soon back in England she would be found guilty by default. Crossing the Alps in winter was no fun. She managed it, though at a cost to her health.

In fact a whole series of legal episodes would follow, concerning where and how she should be tried. And at the same time she was subjected to blackmail – but as that was blackmail by a Cornish actor, you will find it in the next chapter.

Hervey had inherited his title in 1775, so if Elizabeth was not Dowager Duchess of Kingston she was the Countess of Bristol.

Ultimately it was decided her trial should be before the House of Lords, but their chamber in the old palace was very small, and interest in the trial was huge. Consequently Westminster Hall itself was fitted out for 4000 spectators, who paid for tickets.

Even the windows along the route to the Hall were rented out at a guinea each, as at a Coronation. The trial was in part a technical dispute between the ecclesiastical courts (which had declared the marriage non-existent) and the common lawyers. The first few days were excruciatingly dull, but on day five things livened up and Elizabeth was found guilty.

What next? A commoner would have been branded in the hand, but her lawyers successfully argued that this could not be done to a guilty peeress. In fact there was *no* punishment to which she could be sentenced. 'Your Grace is free to leave the Court' – and she did, very swiftly, heading first to Calais, then to Russia where Catherine the Great found her amusing. Elizabeth bought an estate in Estonia – calling it 'Chudleigh' of course.

In Paris she also bought a couple of estates, one of them formerly owned by the king's brother and including a house with 300 beds.

Hervey tried again for divorce, but died before the case came to court. The long story of Elizabeth's absurdly extravagant later years is told in a 2003 biography by Claire Gervat.

Suffice to say that on 26 August 1788 Elizabeth sat down in an armchair, downed a couple of large glasses of madeira, held her attendant's hand, and died peacefully. Not a bad way to go.

Stump up now!

Samuel Foote (1721-1777) was the son of a Truro lawyer and MP. Foote failed to complete his Oxford degree course and then neglected his training in the law. He attempted numerous business ventures with equal incompetence.

Before long he and his wife (whose dowry he had rapidly wasted) spent several months in a London debtors' prison. When this happened a second time, they separated. Somehow he was released, and decided to be an actor. Having failed as a tragedian, he turned to comic satire, and this time had a success; for 20 years from 1746 he lampooned well known public figures on stage, and sometimes his shows were hits.

In 1766 he unwisely accepted a challenge to ride the Duke of York's most unruly horse, fell and fractured a leg, and had to have it amputated. The Duke in repentance allowed Foote to rent and then to buy the Haymarket theatre, and Foote continued to act, making positive use of his alternative wooden legs – one plain, one ornate and gartered.

Like everyone else in London he was aware of the Duchess of Kingston's woes, and also had some unnamed source of information in the Duchess's household. He wrote a play entitled *A Trip to Calais*, in which a character called Lady Kitty Crocodile (crocodile tears…) was based in the most malicious manner possible on the Duchess. Then he alerted her through a third party that the play would soon be performed at the Haymarket.

The story told by a journalist after her death is that she called Foote in, he read parts of the play aloud, and she exclaimed in a passion, 'This is scandalous, Mr Foote! why, what a wretch you have made me!' He replied, 'You! This is not designed for your Grace; it is not *you!*'

He left the play with her to read in full, and the next morning returned by appointment. She asked how much he required to suppress the play. He thought £2000 might be enough to cover his losses – a quite extraordinary amount. They haggled, and she was prepared to pay £1600.

> This yielding only induced Foote to think he should finally succeed, until by grasping at too much, he overstood his market, and lost everything.

The journalist, now pretends to be on the side of the Duchess:

> Instead of a pistol, he had a libel in his hand; this he presented to the bosom of a female, and threatened to direct the contents to her heart, unless she delivered to him TWO THOUSAND POUNDS.

Foote didn't just fail to get his blackmail money: through the influence of her friends the play was banned by the Lord Chamberlain, and veiled accusations that Foote was a homosexual appeared in *The Public Ledger* (a journal first published in 1760 and still running) and in a pamphlet attacking 'the Devil upon Two Sticks'. Soon after that, Foote's coachman accused him of sexual assault. Whilst he was ultimately acquitted on what was almost certainly a trumped up charge, it was effectively the end of his career.

Perdita, the lost woman

Mary Robinson (1757-1800) was known as Perdita – 'the lost woman' – from famously playing that part in a play. She had an extraordinarily eventful life and managed to scandalise High Society in two very different ways.

She was born Mary Darby, the daughter of a wealthy Bristol merchant (though there was a rumour, which she never denied, that her godparent Lord Northington was her real father) and was brought up in luxury. Nicholas Darby was usually away in America, and her mother was very indulgent. In her own memoirs, Mary wrote: 'In my early days my father was prosperous and my mother was the happiest of wives…' But then:

> a scheme was suggested to my father, as wild and romantic as it was perilous to hazard, which was no less than that of establishing a whale fishery on the coast of Labrador; and of civilizing the Esquimaux Indians in order to employ them in the extensive undertaking.

In the event the Inuit did not see this project in quite the same light. They destroyed the settlement.

Along with other financial disasters this led to the sale of the Bristol house, and a move to London. In Bristol Mary had been educated at Hannah More's school where she acquired an interest in the theatre, then in London she spent a year at a very unusual school where the girls were taught subjects normally reserved for boys, rather than 'accomplishments'.

But Meribah Lorrington, who ran the school, was an alcoholic: the school closed and Meribah died in Chelsea workhouse.

Meanwhile Nicholas Darby (who had taken a mistress with him to Labrador) had ceased making regular payments to his family. To make ends meet, Mary's mother opened her own school, with Mary as a junior teacher. When her father heard of this he was appalled! How could his wife reveal so publicly his lack of support for the family? He caused the school to be closed.

Mary now considered a stage career: this was one of the few ways a woman could respectably earn money, except that respectability was notoriously hard for an actress to maintain. Through acquaintances including Dr Johnson, Mary was introduced to the actor/impresario David Garrick, who agreed to coach her to play Cordelia to his Lear. She was now 14, had a good voice and was clearly already attractive and looked older: she had received her first marriage proposal when aged 13! Garrick thought it essential that she went frequently to his theatre to observe other actresses, and of course sitting in a box there brought her to the notice of every rake in Georgian London.

> Every attention which was now paid to me augmented my dear mother's apprehensions. She fancied every man a seducer, and every hour an hour of accumulating peril!

And in this her mother was undoubtedly correct. Alas, her solution was not. She pressed Mary into marrying a solicitor's apprentice, Thomas Robinson. He had good prospects from a Bristolian uncle, who was a successful tailor now with landed estates in South Wales. (Mary dropped a note to Garrick to say thanks, but no thanks.) They were married at St Martin in the Fields on 12 April 1773 – but Robinson wanted the marriage kept secret.

Then the truth emerged. He was *not* the nephew of the Bristolian tailor, but rather his illegitimate son – and he had a legitimate brother who was likely to inherit. However, Thomas Robinson had that sense of financial entitlement which so many people had in the eighteenth century (not least Mary!) and he had begun to build up debts.

By this time Mary had become an expert at flirtation, and made an immediate conquest of her husband's uncle-father, as well as extracting cash from a Jewish money-lender, John King – who had her flirtatious letters to him published eight years later, when she had still not re-paid a loan he had made.

The couple spent money they did not have on a flashy carriage as well as a fashionably furnished house, fabulous dresses for Mary, and social activity.

Among her many other admirers, the delightful Lord Lyttelton decided to seduce her by a mixture of flattery, treating her as a child, ruining her husband by taking him to gambling dens and brothels, and finally alerting her to the identity of one of her husband's several mistresses. From that point her marriage was a sham, and Mary was well aware of the need to bring in an income by whatever means. A contemporary account said that Mary and Lyttelton:

> were continually together at every place of amusement; and the husband trudges after them, as stupid and as tranquil as any brute of the cornuted creation [horns implying a cuckold]

Mary's first child was born in South Wales in October 1774, while the couple were on the run from debt-collectors. Mary was not yet 17: most unusually for the time, she opted to breastfeed her baby.

Before long Mr Robinson was arrested for a £1200 debt, and Mary voluntarily accompanied him to the Fleet prison for 15 months – where she wrote poetry.

When her first book of poems was published, she sent a copy (in the hands of her captivating younger brother) to the renowned Georgiana Duchess of Devonshire and, improbable as it may sound, Mary and Georgiana became friends.

When Mr Robinson was finally released, he had failed to complete his legal training and had now no way of earning money, but still had huge debts. Mary decided to go back to the stage, this time contacting Richard Sheridan. Sheridan persuaded Garrick, now in retirement, to train Mary to play Juliet, and her stage debut was at Drury Lane on 10 December 1776. She was an immediate success, a fine actress as well as a great beauty, and soon had both fame and a very substantial income.

Her husband and his mistresses lived separately, and were thankful to be supported by her. She had another child, which died in infancy, and she spent the following summer in Bristol.

After taking many parts, her most famous role, which gave her her nickname, was as Perdita in *Florizel and Perdita*, Garrick's reworking of the final acts of *A Winter's Tale*. This was such a success that there was a Royal Command Performance in front of George III and Queen Charlotte, as well as the Prince of Wales, later to be Prince Regent.

At the age of 17 the prince was thought charming and intelligent, and he totally fell for Mrs Robinson, five years older, who aimed her performance directly at him. Love letters soon followed, and the press were alert to the possibilities. Two months later the *Morning Post* wrote:

> Mrs — , decked out in all her paraphenalia…, by those wanton airs, peculiar to herself, contrived to basilisk a certain heir apparent.

All of which was great for the box office. Viscount Malden (who was probably already Mary's lover) finally introduced the Prince to her. The cautious Mary accepted a bond from the Prince, that he would settle £20,000 on her for an annuity the moment he came

Mary Robinson – 'Perdita'

of age if she would become his mistress – quite a good bargain, if only he had ever honoured his bond.

But there was some money up front, both from the Prince and from Malden. Mary retired from the stage, at a considerable cost to herself. Unfortunately the Prince soon discovered that he was not alone (besides which he had himself found a new mistress) so the affair ended – not without Mary threatening to publish the Prince's letters if he didn't pay up. A letter from George III to the prime minister Lord North, released to the public in 2017, referred to this as blackmail, but instructed Lord North to pay £5000. Is it blackmail for the much weaker party to a bargain to require the agreed payment? There are usually at least three sides to such stories. 'Perdita' received the money and went to France.

There she was received as a celebrity. Philippe Duc de Chartres, reputedly the richest man in Europe, set up a lavish entertainment in her honour and Marie Antoinette sent her an invitation to the palace. When she returned to London with her latest lover, the Duc de Lauzun, she caused great excitement by bringing French fashions.

In fact she became in London what Marie Antoinette was in Paris, *the* woman who dictated fashion. It was Mary who introduced the simple muslin shift which replaced the great hoops and trains of earlier years, a style which became known as 'the Perdita, a system of elegant simplicity and neatness which has ever so conspicuously marked the dress of that celebrated leader of the wantons of the age', and which we now associate with Jane Austen TV adaptations.

It took two years before her friend Georgiana Duchess of Devonshire was prepared to adopt what was initially known as *déshabille*, after which it became the norm for the next fifty years, until the Victorians imprisoned women's bodies in corsetry once again.

She also introduced 'the Robinson hat', 'the Perdita hood' and 'the Robinson gown'. But it was not only in clothes that Mary Robinson led London fashion: she acquired a series of splendid carriages which caused envy and emulation.

By this time her latest lover, in a relationship which would last with ups and downs for 15 years, was Colonel Bonastre Tarleton, just about the only British soldier who had achieved fame during the American War of Independence. (His fame the other side of the Atlantic was as 'Butcher Tarleton', a war criminal: the jury is still out.) Tarleton, in the best tradition of Mary's lovers, was a gambling addict already heavily in debt, but also the leader of male fashion in London.

Mary was pregnant with Tarleton's child when he was suddenly forced to flee to the Continent to avoid the debt-collectors. Hearing of this, she was distraught. She immediately set off for Dover (though unknown to her, Tarleton had actually gone to Southampton) without dressing appropriately for a night journey. Leaving the carriage window open, she fell asleep. When she awoke she had symptoms of hypothermia, though it is also possible that the stress had brought on a miscarriage, which in turn led to an infection.

Whatever the cause, what followed was a terrifying illness now scarcely known because easily cured, rheumatic fever. Mary was ill with the fever for six months, and permanently lost the full use of her legs. She was just 25, and the rheumatic fever would cause fatal heart failure when she was 42. Mary's luxurious life as a sex goddess had ended.

But she was not done for. Alongside her acting she had continued writing, and this would become her new career. It was also time for High Society to realise that Mary Robinson had a mind of her own. She and the Duchess of Devonshire both became very friendly with Charles James Fox (which in Mary's case meant that he was her lover). Fox was a Whig statesman who was as near to an extreme left-winger as a Georgian parliament could imagine – that is, he had some faint idea of democracy.

A bitter political division was developing between, on the one side, Pitt, George III (an instinctive autocrat) and the reactionary forces of the aristocracy, and on the other side the Whigs supported by the Prince of Wales, who sympathised with American independence and welcomed the French Revolution, which in its early days seemed to be a good thing.

Fox was in opposition for 20 years: vicious cartoons and stories in the Tory press did their best to damage Mrs Robinson. Mary became something of a journalist herself, writing political verses often under pseudonyms, as well as satire against London fashion and the gambling habits of high society ladies. Her house was a social centre for writers including Godwin, Coleridge and John Wolcot, a West Country satirist who wrote as 'Peter Pindar'.

Tarleton's and Mary's debts caught up with them, and they were obliged again to go the Continent, but by the time they returned (just hours before the French decided to arrest all British citizens) Mary had made a name for herself as a poet, 'the English Sappho', when she wrote under her own name.

She became joint poetry editor for a journal, her co-editor being Coleridge, and she was one of the first to appreciate the importance of the unknown poet William Wordsworth's contribution to *Lyrical Ballads*, to which she gave a positive review.

She also wrote a few plays, but had more success with her gothic novels, the first of which sold out on its first day, not least because it featured recognisable people under fictitious names. Her anti-aristocratic feelings were clear from her novels, as was her hostility to the slave trade, and her strong belief in female education and the rights of women: the *Morning Post* said she was 'the subject of abuse because her novel breathes the spirit of democracy'.

But perhaps her greatest radical contribution was the anonymous *Letter to the Women of England, on the Injustice of Mental Subordination*, in which, among other things, she demanded the chance of university education for women.

Truly scandalous, thought many in Georgian England.

And she apparently failed to appreciate that London was the centre of all culture, having the temerity to point out that Devon in particular was at that time producing many creative geniuses, not least Sir Joshua Reynolds and Coleridge.

In 1800 Mary Robinson, weighed down by debt and exhausted by hack translation work by day, while still attempting serious authorship by night, was suffering alaming symptoms. She was advised to 'take the waters' at her native Bristol, but could not afford it. She asked Lord Malden and the Prince of Wales for their overdue annuity payments. Neither replied.

She died on Boxing Day 1800: other than her family, the only people to attend her funeral at Windsor were Wolcot and Godwin.

Scandal at Saltram

John Parker (1772-1840) inherited Saltram (near Plymouth, now a National Trust property; picture opposite) at the age of 16, as well as the title 2nd Baron Boringdon. He was, from the age of 21, an active politician in the House of Lords, supporting Pitt the Younger, and for his services was created 1st Earl of Morley in 1815. At the local level he initiated many engineering projects near Plymouth, including tramways, a canal and a cast-iron bridge across the Laira.

But behind this façade of a respectable landowner and politician lay a secret domestic drama, which suddenly came into the open

in 1808 when his wife's elopement caused a great scandal – and provided Jane Austen with a plot element for *Mansfield Park*.

As a young man in Italy on the Grand Tour, Baron Boringdon encountered Lady Elizabeth Araminta Monck. He was 21, she was 28 and married to the barrister Henry Monck, with two daughters. They fell in love, and the relationship continued after they had all returned to England. Henry Monck, who enjoyed drinking and gambling and who knows what else, seems to have been perfectly happy for Elizabeth to spend most of her time at Saltram with Baron Boringdon, and over the next ten years they had three illegitimate children, who all took the surname Stapleton.

Baron Boringdon wanted Elizabeth Monck to get divorced so that they could be married, but she would not agree, because of the damage it would do to her legitimate children. The couple separated, and in 1804 Boringdon married Lady Augusta Fane, who was just 18 and unaware of the true situation. As his sister wrote in a letter, 'I do most fervently hope that my brother will take my advice and never lose sight of her being 18 and only 18 and really a child just out of the nursery.'

A son was born in 1806 but the marriage was not a success. Boringdon soon resumed his relationship with Elizabeth, and also had another illegitimate child with a ballet dancer in Bristol. Augusta attracted the interest of Sir Arthur Paget, a soldier-diplomat friend of Boringdon's.

On this occasion his approach was less than diplomatic. The couple eloped. (Paget had form, having previously eloped with the Duke of Bedford's cook.) Scandal and divorce inevitably followed. Although, in court, Boringdon was presented as the innocent victim, the scandal-reading public soon knew better.

You might find it hard to believe, but the sequel was very different: both partners were happy!

Augusta married Paget immediately after the Act of Parliament for divorce had been obtained. They had seven children. Boringdon married Frances Talbot a few months later, and she was happy to include Boringdon's four sons, three of them illegitimate, in the family, along with their own son and daughter.

It was a contented and conventional family and the 1st Earl of Saltram was once again accepted in society and in politics as an entirely respectable person.

Sexual scandals recommenced In 1963

Not many scandals among the ruling classes made it into the press during the Victorian period or the first half of the twentieth century. Perhaps people were more discreet. Just possibly they were better behaved – though there were more prostitutes in Victorian Britain than ever before or since – but the failure of the press to trumpet what was known of Edward Prince of Wales, or of Lloyd George, suggests press caution. Perhaps the press shared the widespread fear that the Empire would collapse if its subject peoples knew what really went on.

All that stopped in 1963 with the Profumo case. By this time 'demi-reps' had become 'good-time girls' and actresses had given way to 'models'.

Looking back now, with the benefit of government documents

released in 2013, the greatest scandal in the Profumo case was *not* its sexual aspects, but the appalling and deliberately orchestrated miscarriage of justice inflicted on Devonian Stephen Ward.

Ward (1912-1963) was brought up in Torquay, where his father was a vicar. After attending a Dorset public school, and achieving little, he had a series of casual jobs before studying in America to become an osteopath. He practised in Torquay before the war, and after the war had a highly successful practice in London, his clients including Paul Getty, Winston Churchill, Liz Taylor, the Maharajah of Baroda, Frank Sinatra and Danny Kaye. He was also an amateur artist, and painted portraits including of Princess Margaret and John Betjeman.

When Lord Astor found his osteopathy useful following a hunting fall, he allowed Ward to use a 'cottage' on the Cliveden estate, including use of the Cliveden swimming pool. The Astors entertained widely at their great country house.

Ward's own sexual tastes are unclear, perhaps voyeuristic but undoubtedly 'bohemian'. He allowed 'models' to live rent free at his flat and at the Cliveden cottage, apparently without any sexual relationship. The most famous of these was Christine Keeler.

In the summer of 1961 Christine Keeler, while staying with Ward, met John Profumo, the Secretary of State for War, at the Cliveden swimming pool, when she'd just lost her bikini top, careless girl. Profumo and his wife (a highly successful actress until Profumo forced her to give up her career on marriage) were among the guests of the Astors that particular weekend, as well as the President of Pakistan, Lord Mountbatten, Nuber Gulbenkian, and the cartoonist Sir Osbert Lancaster.

Ward was also entertaining: his guest at the cottage was a Russian naval attaché called Yevgeny Ivanov, who was a known spy. Ward was acting as a conduit for the Russians to pass information (true or misleading) surreptitiously to the Foreign Office, and he had volunteered to do the same in the opposite direction, should the secret services require it. Very wisely they had not taken up his offer: Ward was a show-off who could not hold his tongue, but he was useful to MI5 nonetheless.

Following that topless introduction, Profumo phoned Keeler and paid for sex. She later said that she'd had sex with Ivanov, but that was probably a lie – though Keeler used so much cannabis that she was often rather vague as to what was true and what wasn't.

Keeler sold her story to the Mirror Group, but legal threats dissuaded them from publishing: Keeler lost out, blamed Ward, and later held a grudge against him.

Profumo assured the Attorney General he would swear in court that he had never had sex with Keeler. Meanwhile Ward, chatting at the massage table as osteopaths do, unwisely told an American patient about the Keeler-Profumo relationship. The patient told the American embassy. The embassy passed it on. Harold Macmillan, the Prime Minister, received a top secret minute which described Ward as 'a psychopathic specialist of Wimpole Street'.

And at more or less the same time, Keeler was involved in another trial. She wasn't really that struck with Etonian politicians, but preferred black men, some of them gangsters. There was a knife fight between two of her Caribbean lovers. One of them, Johnny Edgecombe, subsequently fired shots at Keeler's bedroom window, and was charged with attempted murder. Keeler was of course to be a key prosecution witness, but she mysteriously disappeared at the time of the trial – much to the disappointment of the journalists, who had hoped Keeler would blurt out something about Profumo. Edgecombe was acquitted of attempted murder, but jailed for seven years on a lesser charge.

Not long after this, Keeler got into a fight with a friend's brother, John Hamilton-Marshall, and ended up with cuts and bruises. He acknowledged he was responsible. But the Metropolitan Police saw it as a chance to ensnare another of Keeler's black lovers, 'Lucky' Gordon. She was persuaded to lead him into a trap, and to lie on oath in court that *this* was the man who had injured her. The police got their man on a charge of GBH – though that was not the end of the matter.

Macmillan should have asked Profumo to resign, but did not do so. He had recently botched his response to another scandal, and a ministerial resignation was undesirable. On 22 March the story broke. Profumo made a statement to the Commons that 'there was no impropriety whatsover in my acquaintanceship with Miss Keeler.' The Tories rallied behind him, unwilling to believe that one of their MPs would lie to the House. Inevitably it would all come out in the end. But not yet.

The Home Secretary Henry Brooke had a simplistic puritan attitude and believed his job was to uphold standards of morality: he saw Ward rather than Profumo as the man to go for. Brooke was annoyed to find there were no grounds for prosecution under the Official Secrets Act.

Instead, he set the Metropolitan Police the task of finding a crime which could be pinned on Ward, and they picked 'living on immoral earnings'. The Met in those days had their own methods, many of which they used in this case: questioning potential witnesses for hours, even days, then presenting them with an invented 'statement' at two in the morning, imprisoning them on minor charges unless they co-operated, and in this case psychologically manipulating Keeler.

Lord Astor, it turned out, had given Keeler and Mandy Rice-Davies a cheque for rent of a flat, and they had subsequently had sex with men there. So under the carelessly drafted law at the time, Lord Astor could have been prosecuted for keeping a brothel.

But Lord Astor was not the target. It was Ward who must be nailed.

When Ward's trial began in July 1963 it soon became clear that the prosecution and judge would be as relentless as the police. Evidence was selectively presented, or suppressed, and the case depended entirely on Keeler's evidence. The judge's summing up was biassed – and omitted the fact that, while the Prosecution was giving its final argument, Lucky Gordon had been released on appeal after a hearing lasting just nine minutes, because Keeler had committed perjury under police pressure. (Lord Parker in the Court of Appeal deliberately avoided actually saying that her evidence was untrue, though that was perfectly obvious and she was subsequently prosecuted and sentenced to nine months for perjury.)

So in the Ward trial, the jury was encouraged to believe that Keeler was a totally reliable witness; the judge instructed the jury to ignore the Gordon case entirely. The clear truth was that Ward, who made £5000 a year (then quite a substantial sum) as an osteopath, had subsidised Keeler and Rice-Davies, not the other way round. But the powers that be had decided before the trial began that he had to be found guilty.

On the night after the hostile summing up Ward took an overdose, from which he never awoke. He was found guilty the next day, in his absence, and died four days later.

The sexual antics revealed in the case were seedy and unpleasant (many of them having nothing at all to do with Ward) and Profumo did not come out of it well, but the truly scandalous thing was that our government, police force and justice system jointly contrived to scapegoat and in consequence kill a man who, whatever you think of him as a person, had not committed any crime.

Shooting a sick dog?

Many of the scandals in this book have involved West Country people not at home but under the media spotlight in London. The trial of Jeremy Thorpe in 1979 for incitement to murder was a much more West Country affair, since Thorpe was MP for North Devon, and the bungled murder attempt occurred at the top of Porlock Hill.

As with the Profumo affair, there is a distinct sense of the Establishment closing ranks to protect one of their number.

All homosexual acts between men were illegal in England and Wales until 1967, the same year Thorpe became leader of the Liberal Party, and even after that there were severe restrictions. Public (and police) opinion took much longer to accept homosexuality than did the law, and it was only in 1984 that a male MP first 'came out'.

One consequence was that even after 1967 blackmail was a serious threat. Another was that gay men, especially among the upper classes, might enter into marriages solely to conceal their real personalities: some unfortunate wives did not know in advance.

Old Etonian Thorpe was a very active lifelong homosexual who married twice, and was quoted as saying 'If it's the price I've got to pay to lead this old party, I'll do it.'

In 1961 Thorpe had begun a relationship with a young man, Norman Josiffe, who later changed his name to Norman Scott (which name we shall use to avoid confusion), rescuing him from a disastrous job situation as stable-boy for one of Thorpe's former lovers.

When leaving this employer he opportunistically took with him a bundle of incriminating letters Thorpe had written to his boss.

Scott was bisexual. Thorpe was the first man with whom he had a homosexual affair, and he didn't really like being a 'kept man'. In theory he was Thorpe's employee. When they parted, Thorpe failed to 'give him his cards'. In those pre-computer days, every worker had a National Insurance card which the employer kept, and each week the employer had to stick in a stamp, bought from the Post Office. This proved that NI contributions had been paid.

Without proof of consistent payments, no social security benefits could subsequently be obtained by the employee.

Thorpe had managed to lose Scott's card, and as the years passed this became a serious issue for Scott, who had mental health problems and was frequently under the influence of anti-depressants, not to mention alcohol, so was often out of work.

He tried various jobs, often involving horses, but for a short time he was a successful male model – until failure to turn up at photo-shoots put a stop to that career. Unsurprisingly, when things got bad he applied to Thorpe and others for 'loans', including writing a seventeen page letter to Thorpe's devoted mother. From time to time payments were made by Thorpe, through his side-kick Peter Bessell, Liberal MP for Bodmin and an unsuccessful businessman. Scott retained evidence of these payments.

Scott's approaches never amounted to blackmail, but Thorpe became neurotic about him. What if he *did* try to sell his story? He was probably aware that Scott told many people – doctors, a hypnotist, a social security official, anybody who took pity on him, and even in time the police – that all his problems stemmed from being introduced to homosexuality by Thorpe, and the loss of his NI card.

As early as 1968, Thorpe suggested to Bessell and his friend David Holmes, a merchant banker, that they should get rid of Scott, perhaps shooting him and dragging his corpse across the moors to some convenient mine shaft. It would, he said, be 'no worse than shooting a sick dog'.

In 1970 Thorpe's first wife Caroline died in a car crash – she mysteriously drove straight into a lorry coming along the A303 in the other direction, apparently while in a trance.

Thorpe seems to have believed that Scott had caused this by contacting her that morning, which he denied, after which Thorpe wished even more to be rid of someone he saw as a menace. He erected a monument to Caroline on Codden Hill, near Barnstaple, and subsequently married the Countess of Harewood whose husband had left her.

David Steel, the Liberal Party's Chief Whip, had been told of Scott's allegations by Scott's new partner, Gwen Parry-Jones, a widow much older than him and an enthusiastic Liberal supporter from North Wales. Not long afterwards she committed suicide.

At her inquest Scott told the court all about their trip to Westminster and its purpose. Fleet Street demanded a statement from Thorpe: Thorpe spoke of Scott's 'mental instability'. Then, as a PR initiative, he produced a party political broadcast filming himself alongside Jimmy Savile.

Things really came to a head when Scott moved from north Wales to north Devon, staying initially in a house next door to the South Molton Liberal Club – and talked about Thorpe to anyone who would listen. The prospective Tory candidate for North Devon heard all about this, and reported it to the Conservative leader Ted Heath, but there was a tacit agreement that MPs' private lives should not be exposed – and Ted Heath himself was widely suspected of being gay – so the Tories did not exploit the information.

Strange things started happening. Scott's GP Dr Gleadle learned that he had compromising letters from Bessell, and told a friend of Thorpe's. The friend said he was willing to pay £2500 for them. Dr Gleadle arrived at Scott's one evening when he was legless from drink and medication and removed (stole) the letters. The £2500 duly appeared in Scott's bank account, but he was furious.

When the *Daily Mirror* later learned that David Holmes, god-father to Thorpe's son, was the friend concerned, they came up with the memorable headline 'I paid £2500 to Norman Scott, says the godfather'.

Scott was beaten up one night by a group of men in Barnstaple. Then he was arrested on a minor charge and the police took photo-copies of his Jeremy Thorpe letters (quite irrelevant to the charge on which he'd been arrested) and demanded to see the manuscript of a memoir he was writing. The chief of Devon and Cornwall CID, Detective Chief Superintendent Proven Sharpe [I kid you not] was undoubtedly taking an interest, and had personally inter-viewed Thorpe about the £2500.

While Scott was house-sitting in Combe Martin he received a phone message – there was no phone in the house, but he was drinking at the Pack of Cards – from a man calling himself Keene. Keene told Scott there was a hit-man arrived from Canada who was after him, and suggested he should drive Scott to Porlock to get him to safety.

Scott accepted, but insisted on taking his Great Dane with them. 'Keene' was actually not Keene but Andrew Newton, a pilot known to his friends as 'Chicken-brain' who had just taken on his first assignment as an assassin. They drove to Porlock, then began to return through a thick fog.

At the top of Porlock Hill they stopped. Newton shot the dog, pointed the gun at Scott's head and said 'It's your turn next,' but the gun jammed. Scott ran off. Newton drove away cursing.

Scott, covered in the dog's blood, flagged down a car and was taken to Minehead. Naturally he told the police all about Thorpe, not to mention the NI card, but whether they believed it is another matter. Indeed one of them suggested Scott had shot his own dog to publicise his forthcoming book.

But there was a lead, and Andrew Newton was arrested. He

admitted shooting the dog, but said Scott had been blackmailing him; he just wanted to scare him off. The police again interviewed Scott, less sympathetically this time. He claimed they banged his head against the wall, denied him his medication, and told him he was just a typical homosexual fantasist.

Newton was charged, not with attempted murder but with using a gun to endanger life, and with damaging property (i.e. the Great Dane). At his trial on 16 March 1976 Newton's version of events was accepted, his barrister making the point that all homosexuals had 'a terrifying propensity for malice'. Newton was sentenced to two years in prison.

Although numerous reporters were present at the trial, it was totally overshadowed by two major stories which happened the same day, the unexpected resignation of Prime Minister Harold Wilson and the separation of Princess Margaret and Anthony Armstrong-Jones. Nevertheless, *Private Eye* picked up the story, and so did the *Sunday Express*, which wanted to know why the police were hushing it up, and 'Why has the case of a shot dog been taken over by the deputy head of the Avon & Somerset CID?'

The former MP Peter Bessell had by this time been living contentedly in a single room shack on a California beach for five years, but found himself being dragged into the plot by Holmes, himself manipulated by Thorpe, who was angling to make Bessell the prime suspect. In the end Holmes cracked, and told the Director of Public Prosecutions that he'd paid Newton £10,000 himself without Thorpe's knowledge.

But the truth was gradually coming out. Bessell told the BBC's reporter off-camera that in fact it was Thorpe who had supplied the money, which he had embezzled from donations to the Liberal Party made by the rich businessman Jack Hayward, domiciled in the Bahamas. (In the Bahamas Hayward was known as 'Union Jack' and imported red London double-deckers and pillar boxes for local use. It was Hayward who purchased Lundy Island and presented it to the National Trust: he must have been appalled to find how Thorpe had abused his generosity.)

When Newton was released from prison, he sold his story, saying he had been paid by 'a leading Liberal'. On 4 August 1978 Thorpe was taken to Minehead and charged with conspiracy to murder and incitement to murder. Holmes, Newton and two others were also charged with conspiracy.

Although he had resigned as head of the Liberal Party, Thorpe wished and expected Holmes to take all the blame and refused to resign his seat as an MP. The trial at the Old Bailey was set for 30 April 1979, but as a General Election was called for 3 May the trial was postponed by eight days in order that he could campaign. He lost his seat with a huge swing against him – but not to candidate Auberon Waugh of *Private Eye*, standing for the newly created 'Dog Lover's Party', who polled 79 votes!

The trial was something of a farce, and in retrospect it looks rather like a staged farce. The judge, carefully chosen by the Lord Chancellor who was a friend of Thorpe, was both snobbish and unworldly – and very biassed in Thorpe's favour. The prosecution case was put only weakly, and it depended on two witnesses, Scott and Bessell, both of whom were easily torn apart by cross-questioning from Thorpe's brilliant defence barrister George Carman.

Even before Bessell started his evidence, the judge indicated in the hearing of the jury that he should not be believed, and later that he was liable to tell 'whoppers'. Carman took a risk and did not present any evidence for the defence: Thorpe and Holmes would surely have incriminated themselves if the Prosecution had been allowed to question them.

Perhaps Carman was aware that he could rely on the judge's summing up to be one-sided, but even he must have been surprised at the degree of bias: the judge declared that Bessell must be distrusted as a humbug, and as for Scott he was a crook, a fraud, a sponger, a whiner and a parasite. After that, you might think that no jury could possibly have convicted – despite which it took the jury 52 hours before they reached a unanimous not guilty verdict on all the charges.

Right from the start of the trial Carman had had an ace up his sleeve. Before returning from California to give evidence, Bessell had obtained an immunity from any prosecution in the UK for fraud or debts relating to his failed business enterprises. But he was penniless, so he had also asked the DPP whether it would be acceptable for him to sign a contract with the *Sunday Telegraph* whereby he would be paid £50,000 for his story after the trial, though only £25,000 if Thorpe was found not guilty.

The DPP said there was no problem with this – but of course Carman was able to show that Bessell had a massive incentive to incriminate Thorpe, by lies if necessary. If the DPP had wanted the trial to succeed, they should have warned Bessell not to sign such a deal. Were they stupid? Or were they fully aware of what they were doing? Carman of course made the most of it – and the *Sunday Telegraph* cancelled its contract and paid nothing.

Bessell was convinced that the whole thing was an Establishment cover-up, to limit the damage to public confidence in politicians which this, like the Profumo case, would cause.

Many people shared his view, and the *Daily Telegraph* said that Thorpe's 'public image might have been better served had he explained the whole course of his behaviour publicly and on oath.' Thorpe was shunned and, much to his chagrin, never received the peerage to which every former party leader was entitled.

A sense of entitlement among the ruling classes seems to feature rather often in these stories.

Jolly hockey sticks on Sundays

Many scandals involve sex and money, but in the Victorian period a third desirable ingredient was religion: what journalist can resist a combination of lust, greed and hypocrisy?

One of the finest West Country scandals, and certainly the longest, lasting more than 80 years, was that of the Agapemone (Greek for 'Abode of Love') in the Somerset village of Spaxton, just west of Bridgwater, a scandal which centred on the Revd Henry Prince.

The late eighteenth and early nineteenth centuries – the time of the agricultural and industrial revolutions which scared people by changing their lives – was also a time of religious upheaval and 'revivalism'. Methodists and other much more radical groups were abandoning the Church of England. Enthusiastic independent

Joanna Southcott

congregations might shout and stamp during services, and 'speaking in tongues' was far from unknown.

There was a widespread belief that the Bible's promised 'Second Coming' and/or the end of the world was nigh. A Devonian 'prophetess', Joanna Southcott (1750-1814), was said to have had 100,000 followers. She declared herself pregant, bearing the new Messiah, when aged 63. Her wealthier followers gave lavish gifts for the forthcoming baby. But it was not to be. She was probably deceived by oedema (then called 'dropsy') or cancer, and died soon after – but not before ensuring all the gifts were returned to their donors.

That kind of scruple never troubled the Revd Henry Prince. He had entered Lampeter College (founded to meet an increased demand for Anglican clergymen more cheaply than Oxbridge) and led 'the Lampeter Brethren', a group of students who irritated the college authorities by preferring self-lacerating prayer meetings to the hunting parties more appropriate to training an Anglican clergyman of the time.

Prince became curate at Charlinch, near Spaxton in Somerset, where the rector was sick. But the rector, Revd Samuel Starky, soon became a disciple of Prince, and Starky's sister became Prince's second wife. They were both well off, and Prince was happy to use their money.

In Charlinch Prince preached passionately, and declared that the congregation should be immediately divided between the wheat and the chaff. Since the chaff included most of the the yeomen of the parish, this was not well received. The Bishop of Bath and Wells dismissed Prince, who was however allowed to name as his successor another of the Lampeter Brethren, George Thomas.

The bishop also soon suspended Starky as rector. Prince rapidly found another position, at Stoke-by-Clare in Suffolk.

> Having to deal with a coarse and loutish population of farmers, whom he sought to inflame with his own revival warmth, Prince contrived, in less than a year, to set the parish and surounding district in a blaze… the decent service of the church was much disturbed.

The Bishop of Ely soon dismissed him. Finding rural congregations troublesome, Prince and Starky headed for the seaside, setting up a chapel in Brighton and before long their first 'Agapemone' in Weymouth. They announced, 'though under veiled and guarded imagery', that the Promised Comforter was come. Prince, in other words, was the new Jesus. He was clearly a charismatic preacher, and attracted many wealthy people, especially targetting women who had missed out on marriage. Prayer meetings were often in the open air:

> They declared – with shouts and songs – that the Son of Man was about to come; that the world was in its latest day;

that the godly few were being chosen from the mass; and
that the wicked many were about to perish in penal fires.

In the west one of the wealthiest converts was William Cobbe, a civil engineer who had played an important part in the construction of the Bristol & Exeter Railway. He had built an independent chapel at Four Forks in Spaxton. How could the new community now buy the house and garden beside the chapel? The answer was simple. Everyone, rich and poor (but especially rich) must give up the world, sell all their possessions, and put the money in the hands of Brother Prince as 'general banker and trustee for all the saints whom he had saved'. The community began living at Spaxton from 1845, but there were still outposts in Brighton, Weymouth and elsewhere.

The quotations above come from *Spiritual Wives*, a fascinating book by William Hepworth Dixon (editor of *The Athenaeum*) published in 1868 and available online. Dixon was the only writer ever to enter the Agapemone and obtain an interview with Prince and his disciples. Apart from this, the contemporary evidence comes from the censuses and from a number of court cases in which the cult was soon embroiled.

Several of these involved the Nottidge family of Wixoe, Suffolk. Five Nottidge sisters had been intensely impressed with Prince and his preaching there and, when he left Stoke-by-Clare, Harriet, Clara and Agnes followed him, first to Brighton, then to Weymouth and then towards Spaxton. Their widowed mother was horrified, and tried unsuccessfully to dissuade them.

On arriving at Taunton they stayed at a different inn from the gentlemen, but Prince sent first for Harriet and informed her that it was God's will that she marry the Revd Lewis Price, one of the Lampeter brethren and a disciple. Next it was Agnes's turn: she was to marry Revd George Thomas, and two days later Clara was told she was to marry William Cobbe. Only Agnes put up some resistance, but was persuaded. All were told it was to be a spiritual, sexless marriage; and that they were not to inform their relations. They were whisked off to Swansea where all three weddings took place on the same day.

These sisters, of whom Agnes was the youngest at 28, had each inherited £6000 in government bonds from their late father, though until they married it was under the trusteeship of their brother-in-law, Frederick Ripley. (Their brother Edmund had mental problems and was being treated in an asylum.)

But on marriage, their money passed to the control of their husbands – and effectively into the control of Prince. With £12,000 from Harriet and Clara, £1000 from Starky and £10,000 from the Maber family, the community was able to start building its heaven on earth at Spaxton.

Agnes had tried to persuade her husband to act independently, then was caught in the act of writing to her sister Louisa, hoping to persuade her not to join the community. Prince was becoming increasingly despotic: he said: 'If you dare attempt to influence your husband again in acting contrary to my commands, God will crush you out of the way.' And when she was found to be pregnant it was clear that she (but not her husband?) had sinned so she was expelled from the community with her baby.

Her husband was glad to see the back of her, so she returned to her mother – though a few years later, he suddenly attempted to kidnap his son, and (in a landmark case, against Victorian norms) Agnes was granted custody of the child.

Louisa meanwhile, now 42 years old and fed up with being tightly controlled by her mother, had not been deterred by Agnes. She joined the community of her sisters and of others who actively welcomed her.

Her escape was only temporary. After some searching, her mother finally discovered her whereabouts. She sent brother Edward, cousin Revd Pepys Nottidge and brother-in-law Frederick Ripley to Somerset.

They broke into the house where Louisa was staying and forcibly carried her off in a carriage to the asylum where her brother had been treated, and where she was declared insane – though it was 'monomania': this meant that on most subjects she was rational, but on one subject – religion – she was deluded, convinced that Prince was God and that she herself was now immortal. However, her antipathy to her family was regarded as a further symptom of her insanity.

The asylum was an upmarket place, costing a hefty three guineas a week, which was taken from Louisa's own fortune. No-one at the Agapemone knew where she was.

After nearly two years confinement she succeeded in escaping, but was recaptured on the platform at Paddington Station. Now, however, the brethren were able to set the law in motion, and she was released. Unsurprisingly, she now hated her family. She promptly handed her remaining funds to the Agapemone, and started a law suit against her brother-in-law, brother and cousin for unlawful imprisonment.

The case hit the headlines, not least because the lunacy laws were in disarray. 'Alienists' (the predecessors of psychiatrists) attempted to show that they were trying to cure the unfortunates who suffered mental illness rather than just shutting up 'inconvenient people' to save wealthy familes from embarassment.

At the trial Louisa's own barrister said that everybody should be free to worship in the way that seemed correct to them, even if it seemed to others the worship of 'a most presumptuous sect'. As *The Times* put it, English liberty extends even to half-wits like the Nottidge sisters.

The jury found for Louisa, but instead of the £1000 she claimed, they awarded her just £50 – clearly sympathising more with the family. (After her death in 1858, Frederick Ripley opened a case against the Agapemone for the return of Louisa's £5728 7s 7d – and won.)

The trial itself put the Agapemone in the spotlight. It was very clear that the locals were hostile to the community, not least because they failed to do any of the charitable giving which was expected of the rural gentry. They were mainly young people living a totally carefree life. Prince had bought the sumptuous carriage of the late Dowager Queen Adelaide, and he was pulled around the lanes by four splendidly equipped horses, preceded by a groom to herald his coming – clearly, in the blessed new world order, it would not be the meek who inherited the earth. He also needed a pack of hunting dogs to deter stone-throwers.

One curious feature which seemed scandalous at the time was that as many as 40 of the inhabitants could sometimes be seen (if you climbed a tree to take a look over the wall) playing in the gardens at hockey – the game was new at the time, so most people were nonplussed. And what was worse, men and women were at play together, AND it was done on a Sunday. The Revd Lewis Price explained that hockey was 'a manifestation of the goodness of God,' which provoked laughter in court.

The next manifestation, called by the disciples 'the Great Manifestation', provoked anything but laughter. It suggests that the Revd Prince actually believed in himself as God incarnate.

He declared that the day of judgement had come, that everyone who had chosen to come to the Agapemone was now saved, and that henceforth there could be no sin. Moreover,

> The Beloved was called upon to revert to being flesh, and thereby save mankind by a marriage of the spirit and the flesh. A virgin was to become a bride of the Lamb. The consummation of this spiritual marriage had to be in public, not in fear and shame.

The community gathered together in their chapel, which by now had been converted into a leisure area including a billiard table. All, including his wife, were enthralled that a great spiritual event was to take place. Brother Prince chose a girl, described as a 16 year old virgin, and in front of the congregation deflowered her.

> He had persuaded himself, as well as others, that his carnal life had passed away, and when a child was born of his spiritual marriage he was overthrown by grief and shame… this unhappy child of Madonna Patterson was the devil's parting gift. Henceforth the Evil One was expelled from the redeemed and sanctified earth.

Eva Willett Patterson, the child, was 6 at the time of the 1861 Census, and remained a revered member of the Agapemone till her death in 1918. But who was her mother? When Dixon visited in 1867 he met Sister Annie [Ann Willett Patterson] and Sister Sarah

The Agapemone complex at Spaxton

[Sarah Patterson], and a mysterious and extraordinarily beautiful 'Zoë' – 'one of those rare feminine creatures who lash poets into song, who drive artists to despair, and cause common mortals to risk their souls for love' who 'sat there nestling by the side of Prince'.

There is no Zoë in the censuses, so who was she?

There were other Patterson sisters in the community in the 1861 Census – indeed there were grumbles that 'the Beloved' (i.e. Prince) had made these former servants the most important members of his household. Their father had been a butler, then a policeman, then a County Court bailiff – respectable, but not a gentleman. After his death, their mother Mary became assistant housekeeper at Spaxton and was accompanied by Elizabeth Weakley Patterson who would have been 42 at the time of Dixon's visit, as well as by Annie and Sarah.

But there was also a Mary Lowman Patterson, who would have been 17 at the time of the less than immaculate conception, and she seems the most likely candidate to be Zoë alias the virgin Mary.

Her subsequent story, insofar as it can be traced, is rather curious. By 1871 she had left Spaxton and was a dressmaker lodging in Dorchester. A few doors away was Samuel Trickey, a tailor twenty years older than her, who had also formerly been at the Agapemone. They married on 2nd October 1871. Had they run away from the cult together? Sadly, Samuel died in 1879 and Mary Trickey went back to Spaxton, where she lived away from the main house. She died in 1902.

The Great Manifestation does seem to have caused a large number of defections, but among those believers suffering disillusion with the cult there was also a run of suicides and suicide attempts, including Mary Maber who drowned herself, leaving everything to Henry Prince.

Lurid rumours began to circulate about Prince's polygamous sex life, but they may well have been the fantasies of outsiders. Indeed, the absurdity of the Great Manifestation rather suggests Prince was suffering from excessive celibacy!

One of the key defectors was the Revd Lewis Price. His wife Harriet chose to remain with her sisters and friends in the community. Price wanted to take his wife away, but was unsuccessful applying for a *habeas corpus*, because his wife opposed it. So he led a raiding party of thirty or forty men, telling them that 'his sole object was the restoration of that which properly belonged to him' (i.e. his wife).

They broke into the Agapemone, using a crowbar. The community had barricaded itself behind furniture, and had guns. They did allow a small group to search the premises, but Harriet had a good hiding place and they failed to find her. The local paper wrote:

Mr Price has obtained the sympathy of all right minded persons in the neighbourhood, who express their regret that this second effort on his part should have turned out unsuccessful.

In the end Price tracked Harriet down when she was away from Spaxton, and kidnapped her. This time it was Revd Prince who tried for a *habeas corpus*, but the court ruled that a husband had the right to prevent his wife going to an unsafe place. And that the Agapemone was unsafe. Harriet was forced to live with her husband for the rest of her life.

From about 1860 the community was less in the news and seems to have been rather more at peace with its neighbours. By the 1891 census, the ages of the inhabitants make it look like a retirement home. And in 1899 the unthinkable happened: the immortal Henry Prince died, aged 88.

But the Lord moved in a mysterious way. The Revd John Hugh Smyth-Piggott took over, and the Agapemonites took on a new life, building a church in Upper Clapton, now in the Borough of Hackney. Smyth-Piggott declared that *he* was the new Messiah, and was jeered out of town. He too died, in 1927.

The Spaxton community continued until 1956, when its last member died.

Subsequently the chapel was used for the making of BBC 'Watch with Mother' programmes, such as *Camberwick Green*.

And after that 'Barford Gables' did indeed become a retirement home.

Getting to the heart of Wessex

When Thomas Hardy died at the age of 87 in 1928 he was the grand old man of English literature. His will stated that he wanted to be buried at Stinsford in Dorset, 'unless the Nation strongly desires otherwise.' By which he meant, 'Poets' Corner??' – and Poets' Corner it was to be.

But a compromise was reached: his ashes would be interred at Westminster, his heart at Stinsford. Apparently it is a simpler and less messy business than you might imagine to remove a heart from a corpse, and a surgeon was able to do so in a few minutes. However, the urn that had been commissioned to contain the heart had not yet arrived, and the surgeon therefore wrapped the heart in a tea cloth and left it overnight in a handy biscuit tin. Surgeons are unsentimental people.

When the undertakers arrived to collect the body, there was a crowd of journalists and photographers outside the house to record the great event. The chief undertaker Charles Hannah entered the house with proper solemnity, but mysteriously took a whole ten minutes before emerging and calling the bearers in to collect the coffin. They brought it out to the hearse, and the funeral procession moved off with the bearers walking alongside. Then suddenly, according to a report in the *Dorset Daily Echo*,

> About 200 yards from the residence Mr Hannah suddenly jumped into a seat beside the driver and the hearse accelerated rapidly away before the astonished bearers, who had not known of this arrangement, realised what was happening.

Two days later, when the heart was to be buried at Stinsford, there was a further mystery. It had been announced that the heart would be held in a bronze urn, but instead, the heart was contained in a polished wooden casket – about the size and shape of a biscuit tin.

There is a tale which may explain these happenings. It is said that when the chief undertaker entered the bedroom he found to his horror one of Hardy's pet cats licking its lips. It had discovered the heart, pushed open the box, and eaten all but the gristly bits. (Cats find offal irresistible.)

Charles Hannah was a decisive man. He seized the cat, wrung its neck and deposited the cat in the box along with what was left of the heart. So the heart (most of it inside the cat) was put inside the casket (possibly along with the biscuit tin) and given a fine funeral.